MW01595461

Single-Handedly Living a Joyful Life

J. Todd Baker, M.A., LPC

PublishAmerica
Baltimore

First printing

ISBN: 1-4137-2606-2
PUBLISHED BY PUBLISHAMERICA, LLLP
www.publishamerica.com
Baltimore

Printed in the United States of America

This book is dedicated to my wonderful family and "framily," who have supported me throughout my life and who have played a significant role in helping God create the man I am today.

Is Anyone Out There?
A Focus on the Single World.

As a society, we have alienated the single community. The most focus we have received is in recent years, with dating services being as prolific as they have become. The world's mission is to "help" the single man or woman find their special mate. And let's face it, those of us in the single world have fallen into that trap. We have often sat alone wallowing in self-pity, wondering when we will find that special someone. We have been through dating services, the bar scene, self-help books, and countless blind dates. We sit and listen to well-meaning friends and family who try to diagnose our "illness." We have heard people say we're too picky, and we've heard countless reasons as to why we're still single. According to the 2002 United States Census, married-couple families make up 51% of the U.S. population. A staggering 33% of our population is single, and the other 17% are listed as "other" families. In a society where the single population is so large, we often feel as if we are the minorities. We venture to church and find out how to find a mate, how to keep a mate, and how to deal with the ex-mate when it doesn't work out. At work we can't participate in the daily discussions about family issues at the water cooler. Yet when marriages go awry, those same individuals envy what we have as singles. Yet those are the same people who tell us how special marriage is and how much we are missing. I have even been asked how I could be happy without my "better" half.

I am a therapist by profession, and more often than not a new client will sit in my office and ask the question, "Why?" "Why did this happen to me?" "Why did he/she do that to me?" Each time a client asks this question, they are seeking an answer that will break them free from their past and release their pain. Unfortunately, many of life's "why" questions will never be fully answered. The question of "why" becomes a trap that lures people in to a life of sorrow and dissatisfaction. You see, it is not necessary to know "why" something happened in order to be free of it. It is a wonderful scheme that makes each person useless because all of their time is spent asking the question, "Why?" The question itself is not wrong, but dwelling on the question begins to distract us from the real focus in life.

Although we don't need to know "why," we do need to know the other four W's. I need to understand where I came from and where I am going, who I am as a single person, what is a single person, and when are people single. This helps us understand our past and learn from it, and then make changes for the future. So before we try sorting out the question of "why" am I single, let's let that one go and start by taking a look at the other W's. I think you'll see these questions are ones that can be answered and will help you better understand and refocus your life. Before reading any further, take a moment to reflect on your life and ask yourself these simple questions—who, what, when, and where.

As a single community, where did we come from? That could be a difficult question depending on how you choose to attack it. The single community has been in the making for years, but it has only been recently that it has begun to receive so much attention. Everywhere you look you see dating games, dating services, books on how to find your spouse, etc. And have you noticed most of these books, shows, and services focus on the absence of something in your life? They want to fill a "void" in your life by helping you find that perfect person, a.k.a. "The One." The world wants us to focus on a supposed "missing" piece, yet there is no one person that we need to make us whole.

When non-singles look at the single community, they see lots of individuals trying to make it through life without a significant other person. They see loneliness, isolation, and boredom. They see a subdued life with lots of time. Nothing could be farther from the truth in our modern day single community.

Our modern single's community is a complex organism with many different facets. Just as soon as you think you have figured it out, there is something that changes and everything has to be re-vamped. Ages can range from 17 into the 90's or beyond. Some people are single for their lifetime, others come in and out of singleness as circumstances change. Whichever way, the single community touches everyone's life at least once during their existence. This is becoming even more prevalent as people are waiting much later in life to get married. The single community has the largest range of ages of all groups in our society. People are single before they are wed, and typically one spouse is lost before the other passes, therefore creating singleness again toward the end of one's life.

As soon as youth graduate from high school, they take one step into a real world. Many of them choose to attend college or begin working on a career of their choosing. Although the struggles of high school are no doubt traumatic, they are no more traumatic than the struggles we have all faced when entering the pseudo-real life. During these four, five, or six years, we begin to get a feel for real life. We develop relationships, think about the future, prepare for a career, and even begin thinking about a family. Although there are many joys to be had in those years, the trials of life quickly approach. As these students wrap up their college years, they find themselves faced with real life and its harsh realities. They experience the stresses of a poor job market, the reality that they won't make what they feel they deserve, the disappointment of failed relationships, and the lack of that significant other. Yet they find the strength to move on and jump headfirst into the real world with very little survival skills and even less of a support network. Many will move to cities where they know no one in order to make a life for themselves. They will begin to understand the necessity of money and the pressures of life. Many develop high levels of stress, which create ulcers, panic attacks, anxiety disorders, and low self-esteem. This age group is beginning the long journey of life. This group needs a strong support network of friends. Some of these friends need to be going through a test at the same time, while others need to have been through a test. They need a lot of peer support and encouragement. As a therapist, I learned everything I needed to know while in college, but the first few times I actually counseled someone, I was panicked. I knew what to do, but I had no first hand knowledge of doing it. That was a scary time. We are like that in our lives, as well. There is a period of "ramping up" where we learn so much about careers, relationships, and life in general. Then we reach a plateau where we have lots of head-knowledge, but no firsthand experience. It is a time when our bodies and minds reach their peak and our intellectual processes are acute. It is around this time that our life experiences change and we begin to utilize the knowledge we have attained.

This age is also where the idea of the Framily really begins to play a major role. Many years ago one of my best friends was married to a woman who first coined this term. I happened to be very close to my best friend and his entire family. I was the "uncle" to the two kids and friend to the family. When problems arose or when good times needed to be shared, we were always there for each other. We rode the storms of life together. One night we were all playing cards when the idea of us being friends but acting like a family was discussed. My best friend's wife at the time jokingly coined the term "Framily." It stuck. For years we were known, and are still known, as a Framily. Many changes have occurred since then, but we are still there for each other. This concept is the fabric of the single's existence. When two individuals join together in marriage they become partners in life. They are each other's accountability partner, go-to person, emotional supporter, and encourager. When there is a meeting one must attend, the other one can take up the slack with the housework and children. For a single parent, there is no one to help out. If they have a required meeting then they must pay a babysitter. For a single person, even things that seem small, such as doing the laundry or running errands, are large tasks. It is a common misconception that single's have more time and money than married's do. What a fallacy. Singles don't make more than anyone else and yet they have just as many bills as anyone else. They, too, purchase cars, houses, have bills, and many of them have children. As for time, they have far less. Regular house chores cannot be divided up, and for many singles there is no help. A typical evening includes everything the married world faces. They are responsible for their own dinner, their own laundry, their own ironing for the next day, taking care of their own children, mowing their own yard, cleaning their own house or apartment, paying all their own bills, and spending time trying to gather themselves together for mental wellness. On top of all of that, they must also spend time helping their Framily. This is done because they know, just like them, their Framily has no one else to help with their burdens or joys, either. The single community is all about give and take. We must rely on one another to make it. Unlike a married couple, we cannot walk in the next room and help that one person we are to be focused on. We must get in our car and travel down the street, to the next city, and many times to another state or country, in order to help our Framily.

The single community then begins helping the millions of single parents around the world. Divorce, death—whatever the issue—there are individuals raising their children by themselves. These individuals are not to be pitied, but respected. This is one of the most difficult areas of a single lifestyle. When things seem overwhelming, we rely on each other just to make it through the day.

As we grow older we lose loved ones. It is a fact of life that we have all been born and we will all pass away. Normally, one person passes before the other, creating a widow. This widow is once again single. Their needs are drastically different than a 20-year-old who has never been married. However, they, too, seek relationships with each other to enjoy life to its fullest during their remaining time with us. These individuals should be cherished by the single world instead of pushed away. The talents they possess should be recognized and the wisdom they impart should be enjoyed. They, too, seek Framily.

There are too many facets of the single adult life to clump the single community together with the rest of the world. It is not a stepping-stone between youth and marriage. This community has its own life and grows in a way that is vastly different from the married adult world. The worst thing we can do is assume that since we are all adult, that we are all the same. Yes, we face many of the same issues, and yes, we often help one another out along life's way, but singles are different. We have different needs and desires.

We now have a knowledge of who, what, where, and when, but what do we do with this information? In college I had to take some basic algebra courses. I realize that there are many people who utilize the skills taught in classes such as that one in their daily careers. On the other hand, there are also many people like me who have not had the opportunity to use the knowledge gained in this particular area. So what has happened to those skills? Are they gone? Have they been lost? I would have to say no, but I can say these skills are rusty. Just like so many other things we have all read, heard, or seen, we can choose to store this information away or we can apply it to our lives and grab hold of a joyous single life. Yes, even without a spouse.

Perception Change
in the Single Community

I have a friend who happens to be the Young Married Adult Minister at a large church in Fort Worth, Texas. At one time I worked for this church as the Single's Minister and Counselor. While at this church I most often worked evenings, while he was there usually during the day. On the days we happened to see each other, we managed to get our work done quickly or we would simply set our work aside and enjoy one another's company. Mind you, enjoying one another actually meant playing practical jokes on each other and laughing for hours on end. In the middle of all this frivolity, he would usually end up in my office talking with me about numerous issues. We pretty much solved many of the world's problems in that tiny office. Although we understood one another on many levels, the one area that he never quite grasped was why I was still single. We would have endless discussions where he would try to convince me how much better the married life is as compared to the single life. He would ask so many questions, and although he had wonderful arguments, what he was truly trying to say is that he simply did not understand that area of my life. He had never truly been single and therefore could not fathom being single and joyous.

The single community is disregarded by many and simply not understood by the rest. Even many singles have a hard time grasping the complexity and intricacy of it. So what is it that is not understood? A single person is simply someone who has not been in a relationship, right? That is the thought process that must be changed. It is impossible to live a life without relationships. Very few individuals actually live a single life, but many people live an unmarried life. In recent days, the media has resounded with verbiage that certain actions have only awakened a sleeping giant. Of course, we know the sleeping giant of whom they are referring is the United States of America. It is time to give life to another giant. This giant has been in the womb forming with great turmoil for many years. The power of this giant could be enormous. It is time to give birth to this giant called the single community. In order to give it life we must first explore the various parts of it's great body. Everyone need not understand how everything works in great detail, but just like with our own body, everyone should have a basic knowledge of it's many facets.

A single person can be in one of several very different stages of life. First of all, there is the traditional single person who is young and has never been married, but will eventually find a special someone with whom they will spend the rest of their life. This is assumed to be the largest group of singles in our community and on average is also the youngest. This group receives quite a bit of attention as these individuals begin and/or continue their quest to find their mate. All of us have seen countless books focused on this age group intended to teach them how to date, how to find the right mate, what to do before marriage, etc. There are also numerous dating services and web sites that offer assistance to this group. Although there are always exceptions to every rule, in general this group has a desire to find themselves starting a successful family and career. They are often filled with high hopes and aspirations. They are just beginning their new life away from the protective shelter of their parents and school. Although this is a large group, most of these individuals are very transitional. They will ultimately find a spouse and enter into the married adult lifestyle.

As mentioned earlier, there is always an exception to this rule. There are some singles who progress in years who either simply do not find a spouse or do not want a spouse. For many individuals that is very difficult to believe. It is at this age that desperation and depression tend to occur as friends choose to cling to their spouse and let go of their fellow single friends. Of course, there is still a relationship, but that relationship changes, especially for close friends. This is not always a bad thing, but it is a stressor. As friends move on, singles are left seeking other relationships to fill that void. Relationships are often formed and fairly quickly broken. Many of these singles feel out of place and often alone during this stage.

Unfortunately, as time goes by, more than half of all those individuals who gave up the single life for marriage end up back in the single community. These individuals are older, hopefully wiser, and many times have a little extra baggage. This baggage can be emotional, sometimes from the pain of a broken marriage, sometimes directly from what happened in the marriage. This baggage can also be physical, as many times there are children now in the picture. Either way that extra baggage is a life changing experience. Although they are once again part of the single community, they have a much different set of needs, both emotionally and physically.

Although it is a grim reality that the divorce rate is extremely high, there are many marriages that do stand the test of time. They find a way through the storms and struggles of life. Very rarely, however, do marriage partners pass at the same time. As you are aware, most of the time death takes it's toll on one spouse before the other. One of my grandfathers passed away back in 1990, leaving my grandmother behind. It was unexpected and sad, but my grandmother had to make a choice. Thankfully she had chosen many years previously to develop close relation-ships with other women, mostly at their church, which they attended regularly. Her family and friends gathered around her during this time of need. The choice she had to make after my grandfather's passing was a choice of life or death of her own. Not physically, but emotionally and spiritually. One choice had been made for her. She was once again back in the single community. She could either fight the single life or embrace it with joy. It wasn't an immediate reaction, but she chose to embrace the single life with joy. There are many individuals just like her who have lost their spouse; these individuals have the same choice as my grandmother. Some of them find a spouse and choose to remarry, others like my grandmother choose not to remarry. Either way, the needs in this community are drastically different than those mentioned earlier.

We now have a basic understanding of the various facets of the single community. This tapestry is extremely intricate and would take years to unravel it completely, but the point of this book is not to unravel things, but instead to begin weaving them together in a different pattern. As you continue reading this book, please keep in your mind the question of how. It will be up to you to take this information and put it to effective use in our world. Otherwise, this book becomes just another dust collector in the vast bookshelf of your life.

Choosing Your Framily

Over the years I have had the wonderful opportunity to work in many different areas. Some of these areas have been white-collar and some have definitely been blue-collar. I have been the lowest man possible on the totem pole and the highest man possible. In one of my most recent ventures I worked part-time in a retail store. During one of my first days at the store, I met a young man who was the Visual Manager at the store. He was a very unique man who seemed to say whatever he was thinking. He was quite hysterical most of the time. Other times you knew exactly what was wrong because there were no holds barred. A few weeks into this job a friend of mine informed me that he, too, would be joining me at the store. He asked me to describe his soon to be teammates. As I described the Visual Manager, the phrase "no filter" came out of my mouth. The next day I told the Visual Manager how I described him and we all got a good laugh. To this day he still refers to himself as the No

Filter Man. Of course, this is usually said soon after he makes a comment that makes us all look down and shake our heads in dismay, trying to hold back the laughter.

I am sure that you know at least one person who can best be described as a No Filter Person. They definitely add an extra bit of spice to our lives. I have learned that many times this is all done in jest and these people would never purposefully hurt anyone. Unfortunately, on occasion things are said that lead to hurt feelings and bruised egos. In our world, we often resemble that apparent lack of filtering in the things we do and the choices we make. We have developed an attitude that is best embodied in an old Cole Porter show tune aptly entitled "Anything Goes." Our society has become more and more tolerant. In many ways this has led to many positive changes that we see today, but there are also practices and behaviors that are tolerated that are leading to the demise of a nation and world. One of these is tolerances involves the willingness to be close friends with just about anyone as long as fun is had by all.

Previously we have spoken about individuals in our lives who play a very important, integral role. Sometimes these people are our family members, such as spouses, parents, siblings, or children, just to name a few. In addition to these family members, most of us have developed close relationships with individuals who are not in our immediate family. Although these relationships are very important for both married and single people, they seem to play an even larger role in the life of a single. As previously named, these individuals are our "Framily." Although we cannot choose our real family, we do have the ability to choose our "Framily." One of the greatest influences on any of our lives are friends. Parents play a very vital role early in one's life, as do other authority figures, but as the renowned rapper Will Smith once said, "Parents Just Don't Understand." We have all said it. And this statement, or one similar to it, will be mouthed by many more young people for ages to come. During our trying adolescent years we begin to realize the importance of friendships and they become a large influence for us. We have all heard our parents say, "choose your friends wisely," well, truth be known, our parents were right.

We do have to choose our Framily wisely, but why? We know they are a great influence, but how? The older we get the more we begin to see how our own behavior changes depending on the people with whom we associate. When we are choosing a job we take a look at whom we will be working for and with. We should do the same when we are creating close friends. Let's make a quick detour though and make sure we understand Framily verses friends. You may say that a short definition of Framily is simply a truly close friend. We all have acquaintances with whom we interact on an occasional basis, and we all have different types of friends with whom we interact on an even more regular basis. The Framily we are speaking of are our best friends. Most of us have at least one, if not several. If you do not have anyone, then be encouraged to create a relationship with someone with whom you can walk through life. Marriage is an all-inclusive package deal; the spouse should be that best friend. For those of us who are single, we have to create and maintain a relationship or relationships that will fit in the Framily category.

So what do we look for in a Framily member? There are many things that could be discussed; however, we will only mention 3 large areas: trust/confidentiality, similarities, and mutuality. Let's start with the largest and most important area of trust/confidentiality. Framily members should be individuals who are trustworthy with any information that is shared by you. It should be noted that being trustworthy with information and keeping a secret are two completely different things. A person who is trustworthy will receive the information given and simply incorporate it into what they already know about you. They do not allow it to negatively effect the relationship, and if they do think it may have a negative effect, they will discuss this with you in more detail. It is much like reading a textbook when you were in school. The information in the textbook is only shared with the readers, but it is not a secret from others should they decide to pursue it in the same way you have pursued it. A person who is confidential is also different from a secret keeper. In my role as a counselor, all information discussed during any given session is kept highly confidential. However, there are certain circumstances when that confidentiality must be broken. For instance, if a client shares that they fully intend to hurt themselves or someone else and has a motive and the ability, then it is necessary to alert the proper individuals for each circumstance. A person who holds your information confidential should be someone who is also able to utilize discretion in certain circumstances. For instance, if during a dark moment of your life you share that you are planning to commit suicide, a true Framily member will risk your anger in order to get the help you need. Trust/confidentiality are vitally important to a healthy Framily relationship.

There have been many sayings that we have adopted into our society. One popular saying was immortalized in a song sung in the late 80's by the singer/choreographer Paula Abdul. She sang the popular song, "Opposites Attract." This is a very true statement. We are naturally drawn to many things by curiosity. I remember growing up watching horror films and always thinking it was absolutely foolish for someone to hear a noise and then go investigate. They would leave a safe, well-lit area to go in the dark woods outside the house because a twig snapped. It never made sense— couldn't they also hear that horrifying music that always gets louder before the killer strikes?! Yet, in recent years I have oftentimes found myself wandering outside my house because of weird noises, often laughing and thinking back on all the horror movies I watched growing up. How true is another popular saying: "Curiosity killed the cat." We are curious people and that always plays a role in whom we are attracted to. It is important that our Framily members have similarities that bond us together. It is not important to be the same in every area of life, which would only lead to a very boring relationship. It is very important, however, to have similarities in those areas that are most important to you. I challenge you to truly evaluate your life, including your beliefs, and find out what is truly important for you. In those areas there should be similarity with your Framily. Some people may be asking how to go about finding out what is truly important to you. The easiest way is to take a look at your time. Where do you spend your time? Keep a journal for one week as to your time schedule. Then evaluate that journal and you should be able to figure out what is truly important to you. This is not a journal of scheduled events, but a journal of your hourly activities. You may find what you think is important to you is not reflected in your actions. This is often a great time to reevaluate yourself if your thoughts and actions do not match.

In college, my minor was biology only because I wanted to leave my options open for pre-med and then possibly medical school. I never did attend medical school, but I am still fascinated not only by the human mind, but the biological part of our existence as well. Out of everything that I took away from my biology classes, the one word that seems to stick in my mind is the word homeostasis. Homeostasis is the ability or tendency of an organism to maintain equilibrium between its internal and external environments. In other words, there is a give and take among the various parts of the organism and its environment. This happens in nature all around us. Think of it this way: when we are working diligently outside and our body temperatures start to rise above normal we begin to perspire. This acts as a cooling method so that our bodies can stay at a set temperature. If we begin working and our bodies do not sweat, it would raise body heat and could cause heatstroke or death. As you can see, it is vitally important to maintain equilibrium between our environment and us. We are constantly in a state of flux as we continue to adjust to our surroundings. This give and take is also imperative in relationships. As circumstances change in our lives, there must be a give and take in order to maintain healthy relationships. As we begin to establish a Framily, we all must make sure that all parties involved are willing to accept the natural ebb and flow of life. Some people, you will find, always tend to take, while still others you feel as if you are always the one doing the taking. These individuals are necessary in life and are inevitable. They often come into our lives for a season and either give us the opportunity to aid them in their life or they sometimes aid us in ours. These are seasonal friends and are not part of your Framily group, although no less important. They are very important for our continued growth and maturity through life. Your special friends should have both qualities of giving and taking. You should be able to help them in their down times and at the same time know they will help you with yours. This may be a natural ebb and flow, but it takes a lot of work to maintain. It is easy to close individuals off and not allow their friendship to permeate to our deepest parts because it is much less risky not to allow them in. Your Framily members need to be allowed in and consequently need to allow you in, as well.

Although this chapter is written toward establishing a healthy Framily unit, it can also be used to establish a good family unit as well. The principles discussed can be applied to dating relationships, marital relationships, and parent/child relationships. Society often tries to separate relationships, trying to make everyone believe that dating relationships are vastly different from marital relationships and so on and so forth. While there are definite differences, there are still core principles that should be applied to all important relationships. Strong, healthy relationships are of vital importance to healthy living in all of our lives. We need them just as much as we need uncontaminated water and clean air. We can live without them, but it will lead to an early death, emotionally and sometimes physically. As we continue to explore healthy living together be sure and evaluate your life and begin establishing a strong Framily unit.

Priorities

I have an old house in Texas in need of much repair and even more TLC. Three years ago when I purchased the house, I knew it would be a fixer-upper and I was ready and willing to begin that project. Upon making a few cosmetic changes and thoroughly cleaning it, I moved into my new house. It was wonderful. I had finally managed to move from the apartment life to a homeowner. Within a month or so I began creating my to do list and then starting prioritizing those items. One of the very first things on my to do list was to tackle my bathroom. It was a small bathroom and in need of updating. I began shopping around for a new tub and a pedestal sink along with all the various amenities. Before I could save enough money to purchase everything I needed, I developed an enormous crack in the living room ceiling. I decided to re-prioritize and fix this problem and put the bathroom on the back burner. As I was trying to decide the best way to fix this problem, another crack developed in my kitchen; this one was twice as large and needed immediate repair. Once again, I re-prioritized. Then I needed a new office, then a new air conditioner, etc. All of these led to prioritization changes. You may be wondering about my bathroom. Unfortunately, it's the exact same bathroom as it was when I originally purchased the house. You see, priorities are a part of life. The circumstances of life and our value system dictate our priorities. It is important that we not only know our priorities but also know their consequences.

We have all had to answer the question of what are my priorities. This can be a very difficult question to answer because quite often we find out our priorities in life aren't what we thought they were. It can also be difficult since they're constantly changing based on our circumstances in life. Take a minute to think about the people around you. Are they happy? Many of them are not. Quite often it is because of priorities they set early in life, but failed to understand their long-term consequences. Most of us fail to take the time to truly think about long-term consequences of our actions. It is a strange dichotomy in which we live. In classrooms, training rooms, and offices throughout the U.S. we are told to create long-term goals. We spend thousands of dollars trying to learn how to create these goals and then how to achieve them. We've all read countless books and heard numerous speeches of their importance. Yet when we leave those training sessions, the vast majority of us are in a place in life where we can't even figure out the goals we have for that day, much less sometime in the future. So how do our long-term goals effect our prioritization? How we prioritize our day should reflect our long-term goals. Now we all know that this is not always the case. There are many circumstances in life that cause us to change our immediate priorities due to those inevitable crisis situations. Sometimes we even lose track of our long-term goals or make changes to them. This is all part of life, but we should realize that these changes do impact our future through the consequences of our actions.

As we have seen, when we are creating our priorities in our daily activities we should know our long-term goals. We should also be as aware as possible of the consequences of our actions, both negative and positive. Most importantly, we should make sure they line up with our moral or belief system. All of us have a certain moral code by which we live. This code is made up of family and personal values, as well as our belief system. I challenge you to truly give thought to your belief system. What do you value? What do you esteem above all else? Where do you receive your guidance for your daily life? Although we are all different, I receive my guidance from the Holy Bible. Therefore, my priorities in life should reflect what I have been taught from this book. As I look at my priorities on a daily basis, I can make sure they are truly matching up with my belief system. If they are not, then it is my responsibility to change my priorities, change my belief system, or sometimes admit to myself that my belief system is not what I thought.

We have covered the importance of priorities and how to recognize them. We have even spoken about their origin. If we are honest with ourselves, most of us will notice priorities that need to be changed. Single men are often some of the worst people I know when it comes to growing multiple relationships. For some reason, when a single man meets a woman to whom they are attracted, they tend to drop their male friends. Oddly enough, most male friends think this is an alright practice and therefore follow it themselves. Unfortunately, we are living by the fallacy that we are only able to give our hearts to one person at a time. Ladies, don't think you're off the hook with this one either. Oftentimes, the women in our society almost demand a total devotion from their significant other, sometimes at the expense of their significant other's friends. These actions adequately reflect our priorities. As a single community, we have fallen prey to the myth that our number one focus should be on finding "the one." This is often at the expense of other people. If you are a single person reading this book, then ask yourself if this is your priority in life. Are you frantically seeking that special someone and forgetting the other people in your life? I encourage you to reevaluate your priorities and take a look at their consequences, both on you and on others.

Focus

Recently, I was speaking with a friend on the telephone. Toward the end of our conversation I began doing the roll call of mutual friends that for some reason she had done a better job at staying in contact with than I. Somewhere in the roll call, my friend shared that a mutual friend of ours was on a "man hunt." In other words, she was desperately seeking her significant other and had pulled out all the stops in order to find him. This mutual friend had found several potentials on the internet and had made an innocent statement to my friend. While reading the biographical information of one hopeful online, she had simply stated how much she knew this man could encourage her and build her up. This struck me a bit odd. I, too, believe it is important to find someone who will encourage you and stand beside you as you go through life together, but I believe the question for all of us should be not how we can be encouraged, but how we can be encouraging. Is our society self-focused or other-focused, or to put it another way, is it life-giving or life-taking?

This is a question that single people and married people alike have to answer. We are all wired from birth to be focused on ourselves. Although babies and children do give enjoyment to many with whom they come in contact, their main mode of operation is to receive. This is a natural part of our existence. However, there is a point in a child's life when they should learn that the world does not revolve around them. This is an important part of the maturing process. Unfortunately, this is being taught less and less in our society. Other-focused behaviors are taught through modeling from adults and from constant reinforcement of the behaviors when exhibited by children. Recently, I woke up a bit later than normal and missed breakfast. I decided to visit a local pancake house for brunch. I was dining alone that day, and as I sat there watching people come in and out of the restaurant, I overhead a young lady ordering her meal at the next table. She had a voice that carried and I heard her order as clear as a bell. I didn't think much of it until the waitress brought their meal to them. The young lady immediately adopted a negative attitude and forcefully said that she did not order what the waitress had delivered. The waitress apologized and showed her the ticket where she wrote down what the woman had ordered. The woman vehemently said the waitress was wrong. I knew the waitress was correct and that the substitution that the woman said she had requested she had indeed not requested. When the waitress later brought their bill she said to the woman that it was free of charge due to the misunderstanding. The woman at the table showed no interest at all and simply turned her head and continued to complain to her dinner date about the mixup. I knew that this young lady threw a fit and was clearly in the wrong but received a free meal due to her negativity. On the other hand, I knew that although I had been very nice to the waitress, actually asking questions and involving her in small talk, I would have to pay the bill in full. It reinforced the old saying that, "The squeaky wheel gets the grease." Our society teaches selfish behavior by reinforcing it on a regular basis. We should instead reinforce positive behavior in our everyday life.

Many of us will read things like this and know that we all have a selfish nature inside, but what can we do about that? How can we defeat a monster that is naturally inside? Unfortunately, this is not a simple task. In fact, it's an impossible task. That beast of selfishness will be with us our entire life, however, we can learn to fight it. In time, selfishness will begin to take a backseat and it will become less of a struggle. The first thing we must do as individuals is simply accept the fact that we are selfish beings. Our society is able to face physical enemies, but we are running from the enemies within us. Recognizing our faults and weaknesses is the first step toward overcoming them. Often we try to overcome them by simply trying to forget. Ignoring something rarely, if ever, causes it to go away; it simply prolongs the inevitable. While exploring your life, be sure not to discount the input of others. They often see characteristics in us that we are unable or unwilling to see.

It is not good enough, however, to simply recognize this weakness. We must take an active stance against it in order for any change to occur. There are many different thoughts as to how this can be done. I have often told people that there is no one way that works for everyone when it comes to changing oneself. One of the best methods for changing your focus has to do with what questions you ask yourself. We all admit that we talk to ourselves, some of us audibly, others simply in their head. But what questions are you asking yourself when you contemplate a decision in your life? One of the biggest questions we ask ourselves is, "How does this decision affect me?" This is a very good question and of course needs to be asked, but we sometimes have a habit of stopping right there. Out next question should be, "How does this affect everyone else?" This is where we often have problems. This helps us realize that everything we do has either a direct or indirect effect on someone else. Our decisions should not be made solely because of how they directly effect us.

We must also open our eyes to the people around us. As a society, we often notice pain or hurt only if it is drastic. We see pictures on television of graphic images of starving children, we read morose news articles about suicide and homicide—everything is high drama in our society. It seems that the only people getting noticed are those individuals that produce high drama or live high drama lives. We notice that homeless person we see on the street, but do we notice the hurt in a teenager's eyes because of their parents' divorce? There are so many things that we miss because we often don't care to see. We are often so concerned with our own lives and our own problems that we fail to see the problems of others. The next time you go shopping or to your favorite restaurant or to the airport, keep your head up and study the people around you. You'll notice there's a lot more pain than you realize hidden behind a facade. You'll also notice that as you are busy caring about the people around you and trying to help them, your problems tend to grow less dramatic and overwhelming.

There are many other things that we can do to help change our focus. We can donate money, and much more importantly time, to a worthy cause in our community aimed at helping people in need. Take the time to truly listen to someone if they share a need or a negative experience. Offer that homeless person asking for money a dollar, even if you don't know if it will be used for food. If that bothers you, take them a small gift certificate to a local dining establishment that they can use for a meal or two. Oddly enough, by the age of 30 I had managed to not step foot into a homeless shelter for any reason, including to help serve food. That year I decided to take my entire family to the shelter to help serve a Thanksgiving meal to the homeless. It was a wonderful experience and I received just as many blessings as I had given on that day. Find something that you can do in your area that puts the focus on someone else for a little while. As we continue to practice these techniques, we can change ourselves from being life-taking beings to life-giving people. Life-giving is all about sharing both our sorrows and joys with the people around us by focusing first on the needs of others.

Balance

When I was younger I was involved with the sport of gymnastics. I competed for a while, but unfortunately I eventually fell away from the sport. My love for the sport never diminished, and during college I had the opportunity to work as a coach. I joyfully accepted the job where I taught both boys and girls competition level gymnastics classes. Every event in gymnastics requires strength, agility, and most importantly, balance. This is best demonstrated by the event aptly named the balance beam. It requires that the gymnast mount the apparatus, perform various skills, and then dismount a long beam that is four inches in width. This event is both difficult and dangerous. An individual who has a poor sense of balance could risk serious injury if left unattended on this equipment. As I continued to grow and mature in life, I realized just how important balance is in every aspect of it. During counseling sessions, I began to notice how off balance individuals or couples had become, which ultimately led to their demise. Improper balancing in life easily leads to obsessions. Think about how many people you may know who have dedicated their life to work and therefore lack the balance of friends and family. Think about how many parents have made raising their children an obsession, thereby losing their marital relationship. The balancing act is very often neglected and even more often improperly handled.

So we have ascertained that balance is a very important part of a healthy lifestyle, but how do we achieve balance and more importantly, how do we maintain it? When I first began gymnastics I went through the normal process of learning the basics. Those basics included forward rolls, backward rolls, cartwheels, and of course, handstands. Of all of these skills I found the handstand to be the hardest. The reason why I found it so difficult was because of my underdeveloped sense of balance. I was not a clumsy child, but I had never truly attempted or practiced a handstand. So we backed up, and I began practicing balancing on one leg with the other leg at a parallel with the ground and my body leaned forward. As I continued to practice this position, I realized a few things about balance. The first thing I realized was that it is easier to balance with my eyes open. This principle is the same in life. Too many times we do not recognize the areas in which we are unbalanced because we choose not to notice them. We purposefully close our eyes to certain areas of our life in order to avoid dealing with the problems found in them. Other times we close our eyes because we have found something that provides us with a little joy and we chase after that feeling. Either way our eyes are closed, which makes it almost impossible to balance.

Although keeping my eyes open was a step in the right direction, it was not enough to keep me balanced on that leg. The second thing I noticed was that if I held my head upright and extended my chest and arms out, it was even easier to maintain proper balance. With the chest out and the arms extended away from the body, one is placed in a vulnerable position. Although we all know it is at times necessary to place ourselves in a defensive posture, we have unfortunately chosen to live our lives in this defensive stance. We have been hurt so many times that we think it is easier to close out the rest of the world from certain areas of our life. Over time, we pursued the feeling of security over balance. Placing yourself in a vulnerable position means you must be willing to take the punishment that the world gives at times. There are also many rewards for adopting this stance. With your head up, you are able to see the beauty around you and breathe the fresh air. With your hands extended, you can touch the world around you by giving someone a much needed hug, handshake, or just a pat on the back. This vulnerable position also allows your Framily to lovingly share with you the areas in your life that they see are imbalanced. It is only when we know our weaknesses that we can make them strong.

One of the key factors in proper balance is strength. Without enough strength, it is impossible to make all the slight adjustments necessary to stay balanced on an ongoing basis. This is the same with a healthy, balanced lifestyle. It is impossible to live a life impervious to outside influences. Some people are better than others at allowing things to roll off their back, but even the people best at letting things go, do on occasion, end up hurt. It is important to utilize your Framily to help you attain the strength necessary to get through any given situation, but the real strength must come from within. We cannot rely on other people to give us the strength we need to overcome all of life's struggles. Inner strength comes from a confidence in knowing one's self and knowing one's strengths and weaknesses. Once we are aware of ourselves, then we can begin the process of accepting who we are and the lifelong process of change to become the person we want to be. There is also a very large spiritual aspect to having strength. You must be sure of the source of your strength and allow your beliefs to shape who you are as a person. Healthy inner strength then makes it possible to make the often tiny adjustments necessary to stay balanced. With your body in the proper position, you can sense when things are beginning to become unstable and then make the necessary corrections. It takes constant attention and continued effort to keep your life well balanced.

In the world in which we live, we often become disillusioned that a quick fix is a good fix. Although there are some things that can be fixed quickly and effectively, the vast majority of our more serious problems take time and effort to change.

The Beginning

In the first few chapters, we had the opportunity to take a look at the single community in an attempt to unravel the tapestry just enough to get a general idea of how it is woven together. We then took a step away from the tapestry in order to take a look at the overall view of this masterpiece. We also learned that this community was not born yesterday, yet it is in many ways still in its infant stages. The intricacy of each weave in this work is masterfully done, sometimes by individual choice and that choice's consequence, and sometimes by nature. As the world looks at the piece of art, many people see a disheveled throw rug that should be tossed out so that a new one can be put in its place. Others look at it and see its beauty, but unfortunately cannot fathom how it is made. Still others see it simply as a work of art that they simply cannot understand. Everyone at some time in their life has had the opportunity to participate in the making of this tapestry called the single community. It is not that we have all had the opportunity to participate, but how we choose to participate. We choose either to contribute by adding another brilliantly colored loop or instead to tear the fabric by being self-focused and not being attentive to those around us.

In the last several chapters we had a wonderful opportunity to evaluate our own lives and learn about our individual strengths and weaknesses. These chapters were all focused on learning how to become more aware of others. Before we can truly be cognizant of other people and their needs, we must first understand ourselves and our own needs. We must recognize the difference between needs and wants and learn how to set goals to achieve them both. However, it is more important to see the needs of others and set goals to help them achieve those needs. It has become a cutthroat society, with everyone scrambling for the top position. However, this lifestyle will only lead to pain and heartbreak in many people's lives. Know who you are and know how you can help others.

While this book is yet another self-help book, it has a higher purpose. Today's culture has created a small niche in which the single community at large has been placed. In this small niche, singles of all shapes, sizes, colors, nationalities, and lifestyles have been placed. Singles represented from all stages of life are present, as well. With the single population growing, this small niche can no longer contain our community. The single population is a definite culture that must be recognized in its totality. In the last several years we have seen various character traits from our culture appear in various forms throughout the world. Unfortunately, the character traits shown barely touch the surface of this great community. These traits are assumed by the outside world to be representative of all who live in this small niche. To some, we are thought of as sex-crazed beings who are incapable of love. Others view us as depressed individuals who can't seem to find "The One." Still others wrongly believe we are carefree people who have the money and time to do anything we desire. Although, as with every culture, there are some people who do find themselves in these categories as singles, the reality is that the vast majority of us are somewhere in between.

The single culture has much wisdom and knowledge that needs to be shared with the rest of the world. Knowledge emanates from two very opposite places; some knowledge is learned through life experience while another kind is given from above. Where these merge together we find true wisdom. There are many individuals with whom I have had the pleasure of speaking who are able to impart this true wisdom. One person I have had the privilege of knowing for fifteen years. Over the years, I have seen her mature and blossom into a woman of great wisdom. The other person is a woman who has raised a family of her own and has seen the passing of her husband. She has had a tremendous influence on my life, as she is my grandmother. I would like to share some words of encouragement and wisdom imparted by these wonderful women.

"It is imperative to keep our focus. You've probably heard the adage, 'Life is a journey, not a destination.' Well, it's true! Life IS a journey, and a wonderful one at that.

"I decided a while back to focus my life on doing good things—with whatever I had been given at the time. This has helped me a lot during my single years. I have always wanted a family of my own some day, but I decided that while I was waiting for that to happen in my life, I would be out doing good things! So I focused on ways I could serve others, better myself, and expand my horizons. I took night classes at a university, traveled to places I'd always wanted to see, was active in my church responsibilities, and made time for friends. All the while, I was feeling content about my life, because I was happy with myself! Although I still hoped for my own family some day, I was happy in the meantime.

"When I finally did meet the man who became my fiancé, what attracted me most to him was his contentment with life and his confidence in himself. He saw the same attitude in me. We were two people contented with life, and yet still hoping for something more. Now we feel an added dimension of contentment and joy through our relationship with each other.

"Happiness is not something that others can make you feel; it originates from within yourself. If you are not content with yourself, you will not be content in any relationship. So find something good to get involved in! Do something you've always wanted to do! Make someone else's day a little brighter! It will lift your spirits (and others') and help you feel even better about yourself. Make good use of your single time! You have a lot to offer..."

—DeAnna

"We had been married fifty-two years when my husband passed away. He was the provider, and I stayed home with our three children. In 1990, my husband passed and went home to be with the Lord.

"Now I'm living another chapter of my life here in a retirement center, which I am enjoying very much. There have been times when I have been lonely; however, I knew the Lord was with me at all times. I depend on Him every second of my life. He blesses me in more ways than I can mention.

"I stay as busy as I want to stay. I do volunteer work at the Center and I belong to a church close by. I enjoy working at the church when and where I am needed.

"The Lord has been so good to me. I thank Him every day for his goodness and mercy."

—Geraldean

The above encouragements are from two very different women who have never met and who have never walked even a day in each other's shoes. One has outlived the other by forty-plus years, and yet the general wisdom behind both passages is the same. They both share the same key to their joy. They have both found a way to take the focus off themselves and place it on others. They have changed their purpose in life from trying to satisfy their own needs to working to meet the needs of all those around them. What a lesson we can all learn from these two remarkable women.

As this book closes, I encourage you to become involved in meeting the needs of others. I also encourage you to play a role in changing the overall world view of singleness. Let's make sure we don't fall prey to the myth that singleness equals loneliness. We must work together to make these changes, both in ourselves and in the world around us. Be encouraged that being single is not a punishment—it is simply a stage of life. For some this stage is longer than for others, but while we are in this stage of life let's enjoy it by being life-givers. Let's make a difference.